# BEGINNERS LUCRATIVE PASSIVE INCOME

## DISCOVER THE POWER OF BEGINNER'S PASSIVE INCOME THAT WORK WHILE YOU REST,"

I0490781

## BY

**Dr . Henry Toosey**

## AUTHOR BIOGRAPHY

Dr. Henry Toosey is not just your average author. With over a decade of experience in the financial industry, Dr. Toosey has become an expert in passive income strategies that truly work while you rest. His latest book, BEGINNERS LUCRATIVE PASSIVE INCOME
 is a game-changer for anyone looking to generate wealth without sacrificing their precious time. Dr. Toosey's passion for finance started at a young age, where he learned the value of money from his hardworking parents. After earning his Ph.D. in Finance, he worked with some of the world's top financial institutions, where he honed his skills in investing and wealth management. Now, he's sharing his knowledge with the world through his writing.

His latest book is a must-read for anyone who wants to take control of their financial future. With easy-to-understand explanations and practical tips, Dr. Toosey breaks down the best passive income strategies that can generate substantial wealth over time. From rental properties to dividend stocks, he covers it all, providing readers with a roadmap to financial freedom.

Dr. Toosey's writing style is engaging and accessible, making even the most complex financial concepts easy to understand. His book is a valuable resource for anyone who wants to start generating passive income and taking control of their financial future. So, whether you're a seasoned investor or just starting, Dr. Toosey's book is a must-have for your financial library.

# DEDICATION

To my fellow businesspeople, investors, and aspirants:
This book, BEGINNERS LUCRATIVE PASSIVE INCOME dedicated to you, and I'm thrilled to do it. The result of years of investigation, experimentation, and expertise in the field of passive income is this book. I'm hoping the concepts and methods discussed on these pages may assist you in obtaining the monetary flexibility and freedom for which you've been working.

We all understand how difficult it can be to juggle work, family, and personal responsibilities in today's fast-paced world. The capacity to create revenue without actively participating in day-to-day activities is a novel solution provided by the idea of passive income. Imagine waking up in the morning and seeing that your bank account has increased overnight. Even while it may appear impossible, it is absolutely doable with the appropriate attitude and strategy.

You will discover 10 distinct passive income streams in this book, all of which you may start establishing right now. These revenue sources vary from more conventional ones like dividend stocks and rental homes to more contemporary ones like affiliate marketing and online courses. You will get a thorough review of the revenue stream in each chapter, along with information on its advantages and disadvantages and helpful advice for getting started.

There is no one-size-fits-all strategy for passive income, which is one of the most important lessons to be learned from this book. Your talents, finances, and personal preferences will determine the income sources that are most suitable for you. For instance, creating a blog or producing an ebook may be the ideal choice if you like writing and are an expert in a certain field. On the other hand, investing in dividend stocks or a rental property may be a better choice if you want more hands-off strategies. Whatever revenue streams you decide to pursue, they always need an initial time or financial (or both) commitment. The appeal of passive income is that, once the systems and procedures are in place, the money will keep coming in even if you are not actively working on the project. Your revenue streams start to snowball as a result and continue to increase over time.

I think that everyone has the ability to use passive income to build a life of plenty and financial independence. But, it requires a readiness to experiment, take chances, and learn from mistakes. I want this book to encourage and guide you as you travel this path.

Lastly, I want to thank everyone who has helped me write this book, especially my family, friends, and coworkers. Your perseverance, inventiveness, and fortitude never cease to impress me. I'm hoping that this book may be helpful to you as you work toward your own passive income objectives.

This book is devoted to all the dreamers who aspire to financial independence. May you achieve a life where you may work less and live more thanks to these 10 very attractive passive income sources. When you sleep, let these concepts work for you, and may your diligence and hard work pay off. I appreciate you coming along on this thrilling adventure.

## TABLE OF CONTENT

# INTRODUCTION

Are you sick and weary of exchanging your time for cash? Do you have any dreams about making money while you sleep? If so, you are at the proper location. Here, money works for you rather than against you in the realm of passive income.

The ultimate objective for many individuals pursuing financial independence is passive income. It's a method to make money without working for it directly, giving you more time to do the things you like. Yet with so many options for passive income, it may be difficult to know where to begin.

The phrase "passive income" has been much more well-known recently, and for good reason. Simply, it's money that you get without actively seeking it out. Every aspirant business owner, investor, or anyone who wants to escape the confines of the standard 9 to 5 job has this goal.

So how does passive income really operate? How can you adapt it to your needs? In this article, we'll examine passive income in all of its facets, including types, advantages, and difficulties. This manual will assist you in grasping the idea and realizing the concept's full potential, whether you're trying to build a full-fledged passive income stream or just a complement to your current income. So relax and let's explore the world of passive income as you sit back.

To help you explore the world of passive income and find the best methods to earn money while you sleep, we've prepared this guide. We have you covered whether you're an experienced investor, an internet business owner, or just getting started.

You'll have a firm knowledge of passive income and the different methods you might generate it by the conclusion of this tutorial. With the right information and resources, you may begin creating your own passive income streams and gain more financial flexibility and independence. Now let's get going!

## Overview

Just picture waking up to a notice on your phone that says you earned money while you slept. The power of passive income is real—not it's a pipe dream! We'll look at a range of passive income options in this tutorial to show you how to earn money while you rest, travel, or spend time with your loved ones. There are various methods to get passive income, from buying dividend stocks to starting an internet company.

Although developing a passive income stream involves some initial work, the rewards over time are priceless. It is possible to create a diverse portfolio of assets that provide income without necessitating regular monitoring. You may attain financial independence with passive income, utilize it to augment your present salary, and save for your future. So let's get started with these passive income ideas if you're prepared to take charge of your money and design a more adaptable lifestyle.

# CHAPTER 1:

## Investing for Passive Income :

In order to receive the benefits of your investment without continually caring for it, investing for passive income is like planting a money tree that yields fruit every year and increases. It's a wise financial move that allows you to make money even while you're asleep, generating a steady and predictable flow of income that may help you reach your financial objectives and lead the life you want.

You may make money while concentrating on other elements of your life if you have passive income, whether it comes from stocks, real estate, or other investment vehicles.

Choosing assets that have the potential to provide dependable and regular returns over the long term is the key to effective passive income investing. This can include spreading your holdings across several asset classes or concentrating on high-yield assets with higher income potential.

The independence it offers is among the main advantages of investing in passive income. You don't have to work a 9 to 5 job and may follow your interests, travel, or spend time with loved ones while your money is working for you. Moreover, knowing that you have a consistent stream of income even in the face of unforeseen bills or economic downturns may provide you with a feeling of financial stability and peace of mind.

Passive income investment is a potent strategy for accumulating money, gaining financial independence, and designing the lifestyle you want.

## Stock Dividends :

Like a magical ATM, dividend stocks give you money every three months simply by holding them. These are businesses that regularly pay dividends to shareholders as a way of providing a steady and predictable stream of revenue. Dividend stocks are an excellent option for people looking for both income and growth since they provide the potential for long-term capital appreciation in addition to dividend payments.

Investors must do their homework and choose firms with a history of paying and raising dividends over time if they want to profit from dividend stocks. This necessitates taking into account the general market environment as well as elements like the company's financial stability, earnings growth, and dividend history.

The next stage is to acquire and keep a reliable dividend stock for a long time after you've found one. You may take advantage of compounding returns over time by reinvesting dividends and hanging onto the stock, growing the size of your investment and producing even more income. It's crucial to choose businesses with a proven track record of paying and increasing dividends over time, as well as a stable financial position and a sustainable business strategy if you want to thrive with dividend stocks. You may create a portfolio that delivers dependable income and aids in the achievement of your financial objectives by doing research and investing in premium dividend companies.

# Bond ETFs :

A form of investment vehicle known as a bond fund combines money from several participants to buy a diverse portfolio of fixed-income assets. Government bonds, corporate bonds, municipal bonds, and other debt instruments are some examples of these securities. Professional fund managers that specialize in managing bond funds work to optimize returns while lowering the risk for clients.

Bond funds might be a wise choice for people looking for a reliable income stream with less risk than equities. Bond funds provide monthly interest payments to investors and have the potential to produce capital gains when bond values rise. For individuals who wish to generate income from their assets without having to deal with the volatility of the stock market, they may be a desirable choice.

Bond funds may be used to generate income in a variety of ways. First off, investors earn consistent income from the interest payments made on the underlying bonds held in the fund. Second, by timing their purchases and sales of bond funds in response to changes in bond prices, investors may be able to realize financial gains. Third, investors may lower their total risk by choosing a diversified bond fund since the performance of certain bonds within the fund will be offset by the performance of others.

It's crucial to remember that bond funds do include some risk. Changes in interest rates, credit ratings, and other variables may have an impact on the

value of bonds and bond funds. When purchasing bond funds, investors should carefully consider their risk appetite and investment goals.
For investors wanting a steady stream of income and a low amount of risk, bond funds are a great option. Investors who invest in bond funds with the assistance of qualified fund managers may be able to realize both income and capital gains from their investments. Bond funds do include some amount of risk, however, and should be carefully considered before making an investment.

# Real Estate Investment Trusts (REITs) :

With the help of real estate investment trusts (REITs), investors may purchase income-producing real estate assets without really owning them. To buy and operate real estate facilities including apartments, office buildings, retail centers, hotels, and other commercial properties, REITs aggregate funds from a number of investors. Dividends are given to the investors in the form of rental revenue generated by these assets.
Investment entities licensed as REITs are required to abide by stringent rules established by the government. They provide investors with a practical means of making real estate investments without having to own and manage the properties themselves.
Also, REITs often have large dividend payouts, luring income-seeking investors.
Equity REITs and mortgage REITs are the two basic categories of REITs.
 Equity REITs purchase and hold real estate, earning money through rentals and capital gains. On the other hand, mortgage REITs invest in mortgages and mortgage-backed securities and make money from the interest on those loans.
REITs are a very liquid investment since investors may purchase and sell them on significant stock exchanges. REITs do, however, include certain risks, just like any investments.
They are susceptible to changes in the real estate market, changes in interest rates, and other economic variables that may have an effect on how they perform.
Investors should thoroughly assess their investment objectives and risk tolerance before making a REIT investment. Also, they want to look into the management team's reputation as well as the track record of the REITs they are contemplating.

Due to their potential to affect total returns, fees and expenditures related to REIT investments should also be taken into account.

The chance to invest in real estate without the inconvenience of ownership is provided by REITs, a well-liked investment instrument. A well-diversified investment portfolio may find REITs to be an appealing addition because of their potential for high dividend yields and liquidity. Before making an investment in REITs, however, investors should carefully consider the risks and possible rewards.

## Varieties Of REITs

Investors have a variety of Real Estate Investment Trust (REIT) options to choose from, each with certain qualities and goals for their investments. Some of the most popular forms of REITs are listed below:

1. Equity REITs: These REITs invest in and hold real estate, including houses, offices, malls, and other commercial structures. Rents and property growth provide revenue for equity REITs. They are the most prevalent kind of REIT and provide access to the real estate market for investors.

2. Mortgage REITs: These REITs invest in and hold mortgages or securities backed by mortgages, receiving revenue from the interest on those loans. While they are riskier than equity REITs, mortgage REITs often offer greater dividend yields.

3. Hybrid REITs: These REITs combine the income potential of equity and mortgage REITs by investing in both real estate and mortgages. Investors may benefit from diversification via hybrid REITs.

4th, retail real estate investment trusts (REITs): These REITs invest in and own retail assets such as shopping malls, stores, and other retail spaces. They make money by collecting rent from renters, and they could be familiar with e-commerce trends.

Residential real estate investment trusts (REITs) are REITs that invest in and hold residential assets such as apartment complexes, townhomes, and single-family homes. Rents are a source of revenue for residential REITs, and they may be affected by urbanization and other demographic developments.

The rent collected from tenants is how these office REITs, which invest in and own office buildings, make money. They could be susceptible to changes in the job market and economic developments.

7 Industrial REITs are REITs that invest in and own industrial assets including factories, warehouses, and distribution centers. They make money by collecting rent from renters, and they may be familiar with e-commerce and logistics trends.

Before making an investment choice, investors should carefully consider the investment goals and risks involved with each form of REIT. To limit risk and perhaps enhance rewards, it is crucial to diversify between different kinds of REITs.

# Crowdfunding Platforms: Where Hopes And Resources Collide.

Online communities ready to contribute money to projects or businesses are known as the "crowd" on crowdfunding platforms, which link creators and entrepreneurs with them. With the help of these platforms, individuals and small enterprises may collect money from many people who are enthusiastic about their concepts and believe in their potential.

**These are some strategies for generating income on crowdsourcing websites:**

Make a fascinating project: If you want to raise money, you need to come up with a standout idea that people will want to support. It should have a distinct objective, be well-researched, and provide the supporter's real advantages.

Provide Rewards: The majority of crowdfunding sites enable authors to thank supporters for their donations by providing incentives. Early product access, specialized goods, or unique experiences may all be part of the benefits.

Use social media: Social media may be used to attract more attention to your project and spread the word about it. Promote your initiative on social media and urge your supporters to do the same.

Engage Your Backers: During the project's development, keep your supporters informed and involved. Answer their inquiries and criticisms, and inform them of your development.

After your project has received the necessary funding, it is crucial that you follow through on your commitments. Make sure your gifts are delivered and update your supporters if there are any delays or project modifications. You may effectively raise money on crowdfunding sites and make your goals come true by using the advice in this article.

Where Individuals Invest in Others: Peer-to-Peer Lending

Without using a typical financial institution, peer-to-peer (P2P) lending establishes a direct connection between borrowers and lenders. P2P lending systems enable lenders to generate significant returns on their investments while enabling borrowers to access cash at cheaper rates than conventional lenders.

**With P2P lending networks, you may earn money in the following ways:**

**1. Invest in a variety of loans:**
A variety of borrowers and loan types may be included in a variety of loans. This aids in lowering the risk of default and possible investment loss.

You may, for instance, invest in loans with various interest rates, terms, and risk levels. The risk and return of your portfolio may be balanced with the aid of this diversification technique.

Investing in a variety of loans might also enable you to profit from various market circumstances. For instance, when the economy is doing well, you may invest in loans with higher interest rates, and when the market is turbulent, you can invest in loans with lesser risks.

It's crucial to thoroughly consider the loan's conditions and each borrower's creditworthiness while investing in a variety of loans. By doing this, you may create a well-diversified portfolio that can assist you in controlling risk and achieving your investing objectives.

**2 . Selecting Reliable Peer-to-peer (P2P)** lending platforms is essential for safeguarding your investment and reaching your financial objectives.

**The following advice will assist you in selecting a reliable platform:**
Check into the track record of the platform. Choose one that has a history of producing loans that investors and borrowers are happy with. Review the platform's internet ratings, reviews, and investor endorsements.

Verify that the platform is registered and controlled by the appropriate authorities by checking for regulatory compliance. This would make it easier to make sure that the platform complies with the necessary laws and guidelines to safeguard investors and borrowers.

Be on the lookout for transparent charge structures: Reliable P2P lending platforms need to provide price structures that are clear and that detail all related expenses. Platforms with ambiguous cost structures or hidden fees should be avoided.

Analyze the underwriting procedure for loans: Choose a platform with a rigorous loan underwriting procedure that includes borrowers' credit and background checks. This may guarantee that loans are given to borrowers with a good chance of repaying them.

Think about customer service and support: Choose a platform that offers top-notch support and customer service. This might be crucial if you have queries regarding the site or problems with your assets.

You may find a trustworthy platform that can assist you in achieving your investment objectives and safeguarding your financial future by taking the time to investigate and analyze P2P lending services.

**3. Determine Borrower Creditworthiness:**

In peer-to-peer (P2P) lending, determining borrower creditworthiness is a crucial stage. The following elements should be taken into account when evaluating a borrower's creditworthiness:

Credit history is the basis for the borrower's credit score, which serves as a gauge of their creditworthiness. Lower credit scores are associated with greater default risks, whereas better credit scores are associated with reduced default risks.

Debt-to-income ratio: The debt-to-income ratio (DTI) of the borrower measures how much of their income is going toward paying off debt. Whereas a greater DTI suggests a higher probability of default, a lower DTI indicates a lesser default risk.

Work history: The borrower's job history might provide clues about how likely it is that they will be able to pay back the loan. A lesser likelihood of default may be indicated by a consistent income and a history of stable work.

Loan purpose: The loan's purpose might provide information about the borrower's creditworthiness. A loan for debt consolidation, for instance, can show that the borrower is making efforts to better their financial status which might make them more likely to pay back the loan.

Payment history: Check the borrower's payment history for any warning signs, such as missed payments, collections, or bankruptcies. This can point to greater default risk.

You may reduce the chance of default by thoroughly assessing each borrower's creditworthiness before deciding which loans to invest in. Be sure to go through all of the information on the borrower that the P2P lending site has supplied, and ask financial experts for help if necessary.

**4. Reinvest Your Earnings:**

In peer-to-peer (P2P) lending, reinvesting your earnings is a wise technique to optimize your profits. The following are some advantages of reinvested earnings:

Returns that Compound: Reinvesting your income enables you to earn interest on interest. Compounding, which is what is happening here, has the potential to raise your total return over time.

Diversification: By investing in fresh loans, reinvesting your profits may help you diversify your portfolio. By doing this, you may spread out your risk and lessen the effects of any defaults.

Increased Returns: You may eventually attain better returns by reinvesting your profits. You may increase the return on your investment by reinvesting your profits in loans with higher interest rates.

Convenience: Automatic reinvestment options are available on many P2P lending sites, which may save you time and effort. It will be simple to expand your portfolio after you set up automatic reinvestment since your profits will be automatically invested in new loans.

Before reinvesting your money, make sure to assess each borrower's and loan's creditworthiness. Moreover, think about diversifying your portfolio by making investments in loans with various interest rates, terms, and risk levels.

You may use P2P lending to help you reach your financial objectives by reinvesting your profits.

The first stage in managing your peer-to-peer (P2P) lending assets is to keep an eye on your portfolio. Here are some justifications for why keeping an eye on your portfolio is crucial:

You can rapidly see any possible problems, such as late payments, defaults, or changes in the borrower's creditworthiness, by keeping an eye on your portfolio. This will enable you to take action before the situation worsens.

You may change your investments as necessary by keeping an eye on your portfolio. For instance, you could opt to sell an investment and reinvest the proceeds somewhere else if you see that a certain loan or borrower is underperforming.

Increase your Returns: By keeping an eye on your portfolio, you may see trends and patterns that can guide your investing choices. By doing this, you may be able to enhance your returns over time and reach your financial objectives.

Be informed that P2P lending platforms sometimes alter their products or modify their rules. You can make sure that your investments are in accordance with your objectives and the platform's rules by keeping an eye on your portfolio and being informed about platform news and developments.

Regularly assess your assets and keep an eye on their performance to keep an eye on your portfolio. Use the P2P lending platform's analytical capabilities to examine your portfolio and spot any possible problems. Moreover, be sure to keep up with the most recent platform news and upgrades.

A crucial part of managing your P2P lending investments and reaching your financial objectives is keeping an eye on your portfolio.

By using these recommendations, you may invest in P2P lending and generate appealing returns on your money while assisting borrowers in getting the money they need to reach their financial objectives.

## Robo-Advisors :

Investors may get financial advice and portfolio management services via computerized investing platforms known as robo-advisors. Using information about the users' risk appetite, investment objectives, and financial condition, these digital platforms create customized investment portfolios for them. Robo-advisors have transformed the world of investing by democratizing access to expert advice, facilitating stock market participation for anyone, and doing it at a cheaper cost than conventional investment managers.

Earning money with Robo-Advisors is a rather simple process. Understanding the platform's operation and the types of investing methods it uses is crucial.

**Here are some pointers for using robo-advisors to gain money:**

Choose the appropriate platform: There are several Robo-Advisors available, and they all have various features and costs. Choose a platform that matches your investment objectives and risk appetite, and that has a history of generating solid results.

Your portfolio should be diversified; robo-advisors often invest in exchange-traded funds (ETFs), which provide diversity across a number of asset classes. To lower your risk, make sure your portfolio is well-diversified across several industries, geographical areas, and asset classes.

Maintain your intended asset allocation by routinely rebalancing your portfolio. Robo-Advisors do this for you automatically. To make sure it's in line with your investment objectives and risk appetite, it's crucial to assess your portfolio on a frequent basis.

Save money on costs: Robo-advisors charge fees for their services, which generally range from 0.25% to 0.50% of the assets they handle. Search for a platform with affordable rates to stay away from extra expenses.

Remain involved for the long term: Although stock market investing may be erratic, historically, it has produced positive returns over the long run. To take advantage of the power of compounding, resist the urge to sell during market downturns and stick with your investments over the long run.

A practical and economical option to invest in the stock market is via robo-advisors. You may possibly get excellent returns on your investment by using the correct platform, diversifying your holdings, paying little in fees, and holding onto your investments for a long time.

# CHAPTER 2:

# Using Rental Properties To Generate Passive Income :

A common investment strategy is to purchase a property with the intention of renting it out to tenants in order to generate passive income on a regular basis.

You may get passive income with this kind of investment without exerting any effort on your part. It's like having a money-making machine that generates a consistent cash stream for you without putting any effort into it.

Apartments, single-family houses, office space, and holiday rentals are just a few examples of rental properties.

Choosing the appropriate property in the correct location that appeals to your target renters is essential to the success of this investment plan. After you've bought the property, you may decide on a rental rate that will bring in enough money to pay your bills and turn a profit.

While running a rental property well might be time-consuming, it can also be a great source of passive income. You may hire a qualified organization to manage your rental property; they will take care of tenant screening, rent collecting, and upkeep.

A great strategy to increase your wealth, diversify your investment portfolio, and safeguard your financial future is by generating passive income from rental properties. It's a tried-and-true tactic that has assisted several individuals in achieving financial independence, and it can do the same for you as well.

The Best Rental Property Selection.

Finding the ideal rental property may be difficult, like looking for a needle in a haystack, but when done well, it can be a profitable investment that pays off for many years.

It requires considerable thought and close attention to detail. It is a skill to choose a property that is both cheap and lucrative.

**In order to profit from a rental property, you must:**

The Best Location: Search for neighborhoods with a strong demand for rental homes, such as those near educational institutions, commercial areas, or business districts.

Locate a Property in Good Condition: Stay away from homes that need a lot of work done to them since they might reduce your earnings.

Calculate Possible Rental Income: Ensure that the rental revenue is sufficient to pay for all necessary costs, such as mortgage payments, taxes, insurance, maintenance, and repairs.

Calculate the appropriate rent by doing market research to see how much nearby homes of a comparable caliber are renting for.

Comprehensive tenant screening You may avoid expensive repairs and evictions by choosing responsible, dependable renters who pay rent on time and take care of the property.

Maintain the Property: To attract and keep renters, keep your rental property in excellent shape. This covers prompt maintenance, repairs, and value-adding upgrades.

If you don't have the time or knowledge to manage the property yourself, think about hiring a property manager who can handle all aspects of management, including finding renters, collecting rent, and handling maintenance.

You may generate income from a rental property and create long-term wealth via real estate investment by following these steps.

## Taking Care of Rental Property:

A reliable source of revenue may be generated by managing rental properties. The management of rental properties involves careful planning and close attention to detail, whether you are an experienced real estate investor or a first-time landlord.

Finding the ideal investment property is the first step in managing rental properties. Location, the condition of the property, and the possibility of rental income are things to think about. After you've chosen the ideal home, it's crucial to carry out a complete market investigation to ascertain the rental prices for nearby homes that are identical.

The management of rental properties must include tenant screening. A rental application that gathers data about the tenant's job, income, credit rating, and renting history is necessary.

You may use this information to assess a tenant's likelihood of dependability and responsibility as well as if they are a suitable match for your rental property.

To continue to be profitable, rent must be paid on time.

It's crucial to have a rental agreement that is crystal clear and spells out the conditions of rent payment, late fees, and penalties for non-payment.

Having open lines of contact with your renters will make it easier for you to spot and resolve any potential problems.

Another crucial component of maintaining rental homes is upkeep. Maintaining your property's condition and luring new renters may be achieved through routine cleaning, repairs, and improvements. Having a process in place for responding to tenant requests for repair is also crucial. Good financial management abilities are necessary for managing rental properties. You can assist guarantee that your property is profitable by keeping correct records, paying bills on time, and creating a budget that takes into account costs and projected profits. If you own many properties, you may also want to think about employing a property management business to handle day-to-day operations.

If you get into managing rental properties with the correct mentality and approaches, it may be a lucrative endeavor. You may build a reliable and successful rental property company by choosing the ideal property, carefully selecting renters, collecting rent on time, maintaining the property, and handling funds wisely.

**Managing Rental properties May Generate Income By:**

Charge Higher Rents: Landlords may enhance their income by providing tenants with enticing homes that are well-maintained and situated in busy neighborhoods.

Decrease Vacancy Rates: Landlords may minimize their rental revenue and reduce vacancy rates by properly promoting available properties, conducting tenant screenings, and cultivating positive relationships with renters.

Reduce Costs: Landlords may boost earnings by paying less in maintenance fees, property taxes, and insurance premiums.

Improve Property Value: Landlords may raise the worth of their properties and get greater rents by maintaining and enhancing their looks.

Employ Technology: Landlords may simplify their operations, save expenses, and boost efficiency by using technology such as property management software and online rental platforms.

Effective marketing, solid tenant relationships, careful financial planning, and a dedication to maintaining high-quality properties are all necessary components of successful rental property management.

# Rentals on Airbnb:

Airbnb rentals are short-term lodgings that are available to hire on the Airbnb website. A well-known online marketplace called Airbnb matches owners with travelers searching for distinctive and reasonably priced accommodations.

Airbnb allows hosts to offer their houses, flats, or extra rooms while controlling the rental costs, availability, and house regulations.

**Airbnb hosts should: if they want to rent successfully.**

Establish competitive pricing: Taking location, facilities, and seasonality into consideration, Airbnb rental rates should be comparable to those of nearby lodgings.

Provide superior lodging: Visitors demand hygienic, cozy, and well-furnished lodging. The owners of listings should make sure that they are kept up properly, have all the necessities, and have special touches or extras that make them stand out.

Provide exceptional customer service: Hosts should be receptive to visitors' questions and requirements, communicate clearly and promptly and give customized advice and local knowledge.

Effective listing marketing requires hosts to provide accurate and attractive listings that highlight the special qualities and advantages of their homes. To draw prospective visitors, they should also include attractive photographs and enlightening headers and descriptions.

Keep your reviews and ratings pleasant: On Airbnb, great reviews and ratings are essential for drawing in new visitors. In order to provide their visitors with the best possible experiences, hosts should proactively resolve any problems or challenges.

For hosts who are prepared to invest in offering outstanding guest experiences and high-quality lodgings, Airbnb rentals may be a valuable source of revenue.

# Holiday Rentals:

Vacation rentals are places to stay that are leased to tourists for a brief period of time, often a few days or weeks. Apartments, homes, villas, yachts, and even treehouses may be rented out as vacation homes, among other sorts of real estate. The majority of the time, they come completely furnished and supplied with all the conveniences, including a kitchen, WiFi, and entertainment systems.

Since more and more tourists want distinctive and genuine experiences when traveling, vacation rentals have grown in popularity. With the flexibility and freedom to travel at their own speed, vacation rentals may provide visitors the chance to experience local life in the location of their choice.

In order to succeed with holiday rentals, hosts need to:

Choose the correct property: Hosts should pick a home that is conveniently accessible, well-kept and has appealing facilities and features for visitors.

Pricing the rental competitively: Taking into consideration elements like location, seasonality, and facilities offered, the rental fee should be reasonably compared to other nearby lodgings of a comparable caliber.

Promote the rental successfully by writing engaging and detailed listings that highlight the special qualities and advantages of the accommodation. To draw prospective visitors, they should utilize attractive photographs and evocative headers and descriptions.

Providing outstanding customer service entails being receptive to visitors' questions and requirements, being punctual and clear in their communications and providing individualized advice and local knowledge.

Keep favorable reviews and ratings: In the vacation rental market, positive reviews and ratings are essential for drawing in new visitors. In order to provide their visitors with the best possible experiences, hosts should proactively resolve any problems or challenges.

For hosts who are prepared to make the investment in delivering outstanding guest experiences and high-quality lodgings, vacation rentals may be a valuable source of revenue. They may be a more affordable and welcoming alternative to conventional hotels and provide visitors with a unique and genuine way to explore their chosen location.

# CHAPTER 3 :

# Building a Passive Income Stream with Online Business .

Creating a business that generates income without the owner's constant and active involvement is referred to as building a passive income stream with an online business. An online business is a type of business that is conducted primarily over the internet, with little to no physical presence or interaction.

Passive income streams can be created by developing online businesses that leverage various monetization strategies, such as affiliate marketing, digital product sales, advertising, and subscription services. These businesses can operate 24/7, generating income even while the owner is not actively working on them.

**To successfully build a passive income stream with an Online Business, Entrepreneurs Should:**

1 . Identify a Profitable Niche: The first step is to identify a niche that has a high demand and relatively low competition. This may be done by performing market research and discovering holes in the market.

2 . Create a Monetization Strategy: Entrepreneurs should pick a monetization approach that corresponds with their company model and target audience. Common methods include affiliate marketing, digital product sales, advertising, and subscription services.

3 . Build an Online Presence: A strong online presence is critical to the success of an online business. This includes creating a website, developing a social media presence, and building an email list.

4 . Create High-quality Content: High-quality content is essential to attracting and retaining an audience. Entrepreneurs should focus on creating content that is valuable, informative, and engaging.

5 . Automate Processes: To create a truly passive income stream, entrepreneurs should automate as many processes as possible. This covers customer service, social media posting, and email marketing automation.

Working hard, being committed, and being open to learning and adapting is necessary to build a passive revenue stream with an internet company. The potential benefits, however, may be substantial, giving entrepreneurs the freedom and flexibility to design the kind of lifestyle they choose.

# Blogging :

Writing and posting material on a blog, a website, or a platform that enables people or organizations to share their ideas, views, experiences, and expertise with a large audience, is the process of blogging. A blog may discuss a variety of subjects, such as personal experiences, travel, cuisine, technology, health, lifestyle, and business.

In the digital age, blogging has emerged as a popular platform for information sharing and social interaction. It may be a vehicle for creative self-expression, a method to create a network of others who have similar interests, and a way to position oneself as an expert in a certain subject.

To establish a blog, one must set up a website or profile and choose a blogging platform, such as WordPress, Blogger, or Tumblr. Following that, one may begin producing content by writing blog articles, posting images or videos, and interacting with readers on social media or in the comments section.

A thorough grasp of the target audience, commitment, and consistency are necessary for successful blogging. It's crucial to produce top-notch content that connects with readers and offers them value. It takes time and works to develop a devoted readership, but it can be done by maintaining a regular publishing schedule, interacting with readers, and advertising the blog on social media and other platforms.

Blogging is an effective medium for expressing oneself, fostering community, and exchanging information and experiences with others. It has the capacity to open up new doors, foster relationships with like-minded people, and motivate the world to change for the better.

**There are many methods to monetize your blog. Among them are:**
One of the most popular methods to monetize a blog is via advertising. Companies that are relevant to your specialty may purchase ad space on your site. You may monetize your blog with the aid of a number of advertising networks, including Google AdSense, Media.net, and Propeller Ads.

Affiliate marketing: By advertising goods or services on your site, you may get a commission. This works by including specific affiliate links that go to the product or service in your article. You may use affiliate marketing to monetize your blog via a number of programs, including Amazon Associates, Commission Junction, and ShareASale.

Companies may pay you to create a blog article featuring their product or service (sponsored posts). As long as you are open and honest with your readers about the sponsorship, this may be a terrific method to monetize your site.

To monetize your blog via sponsored content, you may get in touch with businesses in your field or join influencer marketing platforms like Cooperatize and Intellifluence.

Digital Products: On your blog, you may offer digital items like e-books, online courses, and templates.

This is a fantastic approach to making money out of your knowledge and establishing a passive income source. You may monetize your blog with digital items by creating and selling your own or by using online marketplaces like Gumroad, Teachable, and Udemy.

Services: You may provide your readers with your services if you are skilled or knowledgeable in a certain field. If you're a writer, for instance, you may provide copywriting or content development services.

You may advertise your services on your blog or monetize them with services using websites like Fiverr, Upwork, and Freelancer.

It's critical to establish a distinct niche, produces high-quality material, and cultivate a following if you want to earn money from blogging. Being consistent is important, so be sure to update often and interact with your audience. Lastly, be willing to experiment and try out various monetization techniques until you discover the one that works best for you and your site.

# Affiliate Promotion :

The best way for both companies and individuals to profit from their internet presence is via affiliate marketing. Affiliate marketing, at its heart, is a sort of performance-based marketing that enables businesses to take use of the influence and reach of their affiliates to increase traffic and boost revenue.

Simply said, affiliate marketing is a strategy used by companies to increase their internet visibility and connect with more customers.

Businesses may reach new markets and increase sales without having to spend money on costly advertising or marketing campaigns by rewarding affiliates who promote their goods or services.

So how does it function? A typical affiliate marketing scheme involves companies giving their affiliates special discount codes or referral links to use in promoting the affiliates' goods and services on their own websites, social media pages, or other online platforms.

The affiliate receives a commission or a share of the sale when a consumer clicks on an affiliate's link and purchases anything from the merchant's website.

Affiliate marketing is appealing to both people and companies because of its commission-based business model.

Businesses may use affiliate marketing to increase sales by leveraging the influence and credibility of their affiliates as well as the effectiveness of word-of-mouth advertising.

By marketing goods or services that fit their target market or specialty, affiliates have a low-risk, high-reward chance to monetize their online presence and generate passive revenue.

Yet, affiliate marketing is much more than simply a business-to-affiliate transactional connection. It's a win-win collaboration that needs trust, openness, and cooperation to be successful.

Building trusting connections with affiliates, giving them the tools and resources they need to successfully advertise the company's goods or services, and making sure they are adequately rewarded for their work are all essential components of successful affiliate marketing programs.

Affiliate marketing is fundamentally about enabling people and organizations to collaborate on projects that advance sales and financial success. It involves using the power of collaboration to develop win-win solutions that benefit all parties.

Hence, affiliate marketing is a potent tool that may help you accomplish your objectives, whether you're a company trying to increase your online presence and reach a broader audience or a person looking to monetize your online presence and make passive money.

Affiliate marketing is the ideal win-win option for anybody wishing to flourish in the field of internet marketing because of its low-risk, high-reward business strategy and focus on cooperation and partnership.

## Offering Digital Goods :

In the current digital era, selling digital items has emerged as one of the most profitable business options. Any form of goods that can be purchased or delivered online may be referred to as a digital product.

These goods are often available digitally as downloaded files, software applications, ebooks, audio files, movies, courses, and a wide range of other things.

Customers love digital items for a variety of reasons. They are simple to access, often instantaneously accessible, and portable across all platforms, including computers, cellphones, and tablets. They are also incredibly practical since there is no need for physical delivery because clients may order and get them from anywhere in the globe.

Offering digital goods is a successful business strategy for small and large companies alike. It enables firms to produce and market goods without incurring the overhead expenditures of producing, storing, and transporting actual goods. Digital items, on the other hand, may be produced and supplied at a fraction of the price, making this business model very successful.

Digital goods may be sold via a variety of methods, such as online stores, social media networks, email marketing, and online marketplaces. The secret to creating a digital product that sells well is to make sure it fulfills the demands of the consumer and adds value. This may be accomplished by determining a target market and learning about their problems, interests, and preferences.

It's crucial to make sure that digital items are both high-quality and aesthetically pleasing while generating them. Professional design, layout, and formatting may do this. Also, it's crucial to check that the product has user-friendly interfaces, clear instructions, and is simple to use.

Depending on the kind of product and the market need, digital items may have varying prices. As they are often more affordable than physical goods, digital goods are more widely available. To make sure that digital goods are successful and long-lasting in the long term, it is crucial to price them fairly.

The success of the sale of digital items depends on marketing and promotion. Many channels, including social media, email marketing, paid advertising, and content marketing, may be used to accomplish this. It's crucial to establish a solid brand identity and a devoted consumer base via successful marketing techniques.

Customer service is a crucial component of selling digital goods. Consumers must have faith in their purchases and be aware that they may contact customer service if they have any problems. This may be done through a variety of support methods, including phone, chat, or email. Selling digital items is a very profitable business venture that has several advantages for entrepreneurs and companies.

It enables businesses to produce and sell goods without incurring the overhead expenses related to tangible goods, making it a very successful business model.

The secret to success is producing high-quality goods that satisfy the demands of the intended market, pricing them fairly, and marketing them successfully. Selling digital goods may be a lucrative and long-lasting business endeavor with the appropriate strategy.

## Creating An Online Course :

Making an online course is a fantastic way to make money from the comfort of your home while imparting your knowledge and skills to others. An online course may be a potent tool for reaching a worldwide audience and enhancing your personal brand, regardless of whether you are an expert in a certain industry or have a talent that you wish to teach.

You must decide on your course content and target audience before you start the development process. What area of study are you hoping to teach? Who would be your ideal pupil? What issue do you want to address for your audience? You may clearly determine what you need to teach and how to sell your course by responding to these questions.

After you've determined your subject and target market, it's time to organize the course's material.

This may include making lesson plans, preparing slides or other visual aids, and producing lectures on video or audio.

To make it simpler for students to follow up with and understand the information, think about segmenting your course into modules or chapters. It's crucial to keep your audience in mind when you develop the material for your course. Employ simple language instead of jargon or technical terminology that your pupils may not understand.

To keep students interested and aid with knowledge retention, make sure your material is interactive and includes exercises, quizzes, and other activities.

You will need a platform to host your material and distribute it to your students if you want to develop an online course.

There are several platforms accessible, ranging from cost-effective alternatives like Teachable and Thinkific to free ones like YouTube and Udemy. Consider your budget, the features you need, and the amount of support you need when selecting a platform.

It's time to promote your course and draw students after you've prepared your course materials and selected a platform. To advertise your course, you may do things like make a landing page, use social media advertisements, and tap into your current network. To encourage prospective students to join up, think about providing a free trial or first session.

Being receptive to student input is crucial while establishing your course. Invite students to express their opinions on the course's structure and content in the form of questions. This will enable you to improve your course over time and provide your students with a better learning environment.

Making an online course is a potent approach to making money from the comfort of your home while imparting your knowledge and skills to others. You may design an online course that works for you and your students by deciding on a subject and audience, arranging your material, selecting a platform, and promoting your course well.

An online course may be a tremendously satisfying and enjoyable way to share your passion and skills with the world if you approach it the proper way.

## E-Commerce :

The exchange of products and services through the internet is known as electronic commerce or e-commerce. As more and more people are turning to online shopping for convenience and accessibility, this form of business has grown in popularity.

Business-to-consumer (B2C), business-to-business (B2B), and consumer-to-consumer (C2C) are just a few of the several business models that fall under the umbrella of e-commerce (C2C).

Whereas B2B e-commerce includes the selling of products or services between companies, B2C e-commerce involves the sale of products or services directly to consumers. The selling of products or services between consumers, generally via online marketplaces, is referred to as C2C e-commerce.

The accessibility of e-commerce is one of its main benefits. Without ever leaving their homes, customers may shop from anywhere in the globe, at any hour of the day or night.

E-commerce enables companies to access a worldwide audience and increase their consumer base outside of their own geographic area.

The adaptability of e-commerce is another benefit. With no requirement for physical storefronts or inventory storage, businesses may provide a broad variety of goods and services via their online sites.

As a result, companies are able to swiftly and effectively adjust to shifting market circumstances and client needs.

Businesses need a website or online shop, the ability to accept payments, a method of order fulfillment, and a means of product delivery to consumers in order to launch an e-commerce operation.

Several e-commerce systems, like Shopify, WooCommerce, or Magento, which provide companies with the tools they need to build and run their online storefronts, may help accomplish this.

Also essential to the success of e-commerce enterprises are marketing and advertising. This may involve paid advertising, social media marketing, email marketing, and search engine optimization (SEO). Effective product and service promotion helps firms draw in more clients and increase revenue.

E-commerce must also take security into account. While making purchases online, customers must have faith that their financial and personal information is secure. Secure payment processing, SSL encryption, and other security measures to thwart fraud and data breaches may accomplish this.

The way we shop and do business has been changed by e-commerce. E-commerce has developed into a great tool for companies of all kinds to reach a broader audience and increase sales because of its accessibility, flexibility, and worldwide reach. Businesses may succeed in the world of e-commerce by building an engaging online store, advertising items wisely, and offering a safe buying environment.

# CHAPTER 4:

## Using Artistic Assets to Generate Passive Income .

Income obtained without active labor is referred to as passive income. For people with artistic aptitude, passive income streams from creative assets might be very beneficial. Digital goods like e-books, photographs, music, and graphic design are examples of creative assets.

Finding your area of expertise is the first step in using creative assets to generate passive revenue. What kind of artistic abilities do you possess? Do you own a body of work you can sell? After you've determined your areas of strength, you may start to produce digital goods that highlight your knowledge and abilities.

Making and selling digital goods like e-books, courses, or design templates is one of the most well-liked methods to generate passive income using creative assets. Online stores like Etsy, Creative Market, or Gumroad are good ways to sell these goods. It's critical to build high-quality, aesthetically attractive, and useful digital goods while designing them, always keeping the client in mind.

Stock photography and video are two more ways to use creative assets to generate passive revenue. Photographers and videographers may publish their work to websites like Shutterstock, iStock, and Getty Images and get royalties for each download or usage of the material. Similarly to this, artists may generate passive revenue by selling their music on websites like Bandcamp, iTunes, and Spotify.

By producing design templates, such as logos, business cards, or social media images, and reselling them on internet marketplaces, graphic artists may also generate passive revenue. Moreover, via websites like Creative Market and Envato Market, designers may produce and market digital assets like fonts, icons, and textures.

Although generating passive income via creative assets might be profitable, it's vital to remember that producing high-quality goods that will sell well requires time and work. To make sure that your items remain current and in demand, it's also critical to keep up with trends and consumer preferences.

For people with creative abilities, earning passive income using creative assets may be a terrific method to create extra income streams. There are several chances to produce and market digital goods that highlight your skills whether you're a writer, photographer, singer, or graphic designer. You may establish a lucrative passive income stream that generates revenue for years to come by producing high-quality goods that provide value for the consumer and marketing them successfully via internet marketplaces.

# Purchasing Stock Images:

Photographers may make money by licensing their images to other parties for use in different projects including websites, marketing materials, and periodicals by selling stock photographs. Stock photographs are pre-existing images that may be acquired by people or companies for a price and are licensed for a particular purpose.

Photographers must compile a portfolio of top-notch pictures that demonstrate their talents and competence before they can begin selling stock photographs. These pictures are accessible for upload to stock photography services including Shutterstock, iStock, and Adobe Stock. These websites provide a forum for photographers to sell their images to a big audience and make money from each download or licensing of their images.

It's crucial to consider prospective purchasers' demands while producing stock pictures. Photographers should strive to produce photographs that have the potential to be used in a range of projects and are aesthetically pleasing, high-quality, and adaptable. The themes that are often included in stock photography include lifestyle, travel, business and technology, and nature.

Photographers may also think about using relevant keywords and tags in their photographs to improve the likelihood that their work will be licensed. When looking for certain subjects or themes, this aids prospective purchasers in finding the images they want.

When selling stock images, it's also crucial to keep legal issues in mind. Photographers must make sure they have the legal authority to sell their images and that any identifiable people or branded items have been given permission to be used for commercial purposes.

Knowing the license requirements and pricing schemes is another crucial element of selling stock photographs. To find the greatest match for your photographs and your company objectives, you should investigate and evaluate the various stock photography websites' licensing policies and pricing schemes.

By granting licenses to a large audience, selling stock pictures may be a lucrative method for photographers to make money. Photographers may develop a successful company selling stock pictures by building a portfolio of high-quality images, comprehending the demands of prospective customers, and adhering to legal issues and licensing requirements. Selling stock pictures may be a reliable source of passive income with the appropriate strategy and commitment, and it also gives photographers a platform to share their talent and creativity with the world.

# Licensing Music :

Licensing music refers to the process of obtaining permission to use a particular piece of music for a specific purpose, such as in a film, TV show, commercial, or video game. Music licensing allows the copyright owner to receive compensation for the use of their music and provides the licensee with the legal right to use the music for their project.

Music licensing is typically handled by music publishers, record labels, and licensing agencies. These entities represent the rights holders and negotiate licensing deals on their behalf. To obtain a license, the licensee must contact the appropriate rights holder and negotiate the terms of the license agreement, including the duration of the license, the territory in which the music can be used, and the fee for use of the music.

There are Two Main Types of Music Licenses:

Synchronization Licenses and Performance Licenses.

A Synchronization License, also known as a Sync License, is a type of music license that grants permission to use a specific piece of music in conjunction with visual media. Visual media can include television shows, films, commercials, video games, and other forms of multimedia. Synchronization licenses are typically granted by the copyright holder of the musical work, which can include the songwriter, composer, music publisher, or record label. The license agreement will specify the terms and conditions for the use of the music, including the specific visual media project, the duration of the license, and the fee to be paid to the copyright holder.

Synchronization licenses can be exclusive or non-exclusive.

An exclusive synchronization license grants the licensee the sole right to use the music in the specific project for the duration of the license agreement. A non-exclusive synchronization license allows the licensee to use the music in their project, but the copyright holder can grant permission to others to use the same music for other projects.

When obtaining a synchronization license, it's important to obtain permission from all the copyright holders involved in the musical work. This can include the songwriter, composer, music publisher, and record label. Failure to obtain permission from all the copyright holders can result in legal issues and potential copyright infringement.

Synchronization licenses are an important part of the music industry, as they allow music to be used to enhance visual media projects and create a memorable experience for the audience. By understanding the terms and conditions of a synchronization license, businesses, filmmakers, and musicians can legally use music in their projects and avoid potential legal issues.

A Performance License :

A performance license is a type of music license that grants permission to publicly perform a musical work. The license allows a person or organization to play or perform a specific piece of music in a public setting, such as in a live performance or on the radio.

Performance licenses are typically granted by the copyright holder of the musical work, which can include the songwriter, composer, music publisher, or performing rights organization (PRO). PROs are organizations that represent the interests of songwriters and music publishers and manage the collection and distribution of royalties for the public performance of musical works.

To obtain a performance license, a person or organization must contact the appropriate rights holder or PRO and obtain permission to use the music for their performance. The license agreement will specify the terms and conditions for the use of the music, including the type of performance, the venue, and the fee to be paid to the copyright holder or PRO.

Performance licenses can be exclusive or non-exclusive. An exclusive performance license grants the licensee the sole right to perform the music in the specific performance for the duration of the license agreement. A non-exclusive performance license allows the licensee to perform the music, but the copyright holder or PRO can grant permission to others to perform the same music for other performances.

It's important to obtain a performance license before publicly performing a musical work to avoid potential legal issues and copyright infringement. PROs can also provide additional benefits to songwriters and music publishers, such as monitoring and collecting royalties for the public performance of their music.

A Performance license is a crucial part of the music industry that allows for the legal public performance of musical works.

By obtaining a performance license, musicians, venues, and other organizations can legally use music in their performances and support the interests of songwriters and music publishers.

Understanding the terms and conditions of a performance license and obtaining permission from the appropriate rights holders or PROs is essential to avoid legal issues and ensure a successful and legal performance.

These two main types of licenses, there are also different types of licensing agreements, such as exclusive and non-exclusive licenses.

An exclusive license grants the licensee the sole right to use the music for a specific purpose, while a non-exclusive license allows multiple licensees to use the same music for their projects.

When licensing music, it's important to understand the legal requirements and terms of the license agreement. This includes understanding the specific rights being licensed, the duration of the license, and any restrictions on the use of the music.

It's also important to obtain the appropriate licenses and permissions to avoid legal issues or potential copyright infringement.

Licensing music is an important process for both the copyright owner and the licensee. It provides the copyright owner with compensation for the use of their music and allows the licensee to legally use the music in their projects.

Understanding the different types of licenses and agreements, as well as the legal requirements and terms of the license agreement, is crucial to ensure the successful and legal use of the music. By navigating the music licensing process, businesses, filmmakers, and musicians can utilize the power of music to enhance their projects and create a memorable experience for their audience.

## Creating and Selling Artwork :

Creating and selling artwork is a popular way for artists to share their creativity with the world and earn a living from their passion. There are various forms of artwork that artists can create, including paintings, drawings, sculptures, digital art, and more.

**Here are some key steps to consider when creating and selling artwork:**

Develop Your Style: It's important to develop a unique style that distinguishes your artwork from others. This can be achieved through experimenting with different techniques, mediums, and subject matter until you find your own voice.

Create Your Artwork: Once you've developed your style, it's time to create your artwork. This involves choosing the right materials and tools and dedicating time and effort to produce quality pieces.

Photograph or Scan Your Artwork: If you're planning to sell your artwork online, it's important to have high-quality photographs or scans of your pieces. This can be done with a camera or scanner, and to capture the details and colors of the artwork as accurately as possible.

Determine Your Pricing: Pricing your artwork can be challenging, but it's important to consider factors such as size, medium, complexity, and demand for your artwork. Researching the prices of similar artwork can also give you a better idea of the market value.

Choose Your Sales Channels: There are various sales channels available for artists, including online marketplaces, art galleries, and social media platforms. It's important to choose the channels that align with your goals and target audience.

Market Your Artwork: Promoting your artwork is crucial to reach potential buyers. This can be done through social media, email marketing, advertising, and networking with other artists and art enthusiasts.

Fulfill Orders: Once you receive an order for your artwork, it's important to package it securely and ship it promptly. This helps to ensure that the artwork arrives in good condition and the buyer is satisfied.

Build Relationships With Buyers: Building relationships with buyers can lead to repeat business and referrals. It's important to communicate with buyers and provide exceptional customer service to foster positive relationships.

Creating and selling artwork can be a rewarding and fulfilling experience for artists. By developing your style, creating quality pieces, determining your pricing, choosing the right sales channels, marketing your artwork, fulfilling orders, and building relationships with buyers, you can establish a successful art business and share your creativity with the world.

# Writing eBooks :

Writing eBooks has become a popular way for authors to share their knowledge, creativity, and stories with readers around the world. An eBook is a digital book that can be read on electronic devices such as e-readers, tablets, and smartphones.

**Here are some key steps to consider when writing and publishing an eBook:**

Choose a topic: The first step in writing an eBook is to choose a topic that aligns with your interests, expertise, and target audience. It's important to research the market demand for your chosen topic and ensure that it's relevant and valuable to readers.

Outline your eBook: Once you've chosen your topic, it's important to create an outline that organizes your ideas and helps you to stay focused. An outline can also serve as a roadmap for your writing process.

Write your eBook: With your outline in place, it's time to start writing your eBook. It's important to write in a clear, concise, and engaging style that resonates with your target audience. Editing and revising your work is also essential to ensure that it's polished and error-free.

Design your eBook: The design of your eBook can impact its appeal and readability. This includes choosing a font, layout, and cover design that aligns with your brand and target audience.

Convert your eBook: Once your eBook is written and designed, it's important to convert it into a digital format such as PDF or EPUB that can be easily read on electronic devices.

Publish your eBook: There are various platforms available for self-publishing eBooks, including Amazon Kindle Direct Publishing, Barnes & Noble Press, kobo writing life, and Apple iBooks. It's important to choose a platform that aligns with your goals and target audience.

Market your eBook: Promoting your eBook is crucial to reach potential readers. This can be done through social media, email marketing, advertising, and networking with other authors and book enthusiasts.

Monitor and adjust: It's important to monitor the sales and reviews of your eBook and make adjustments as necessary. This includes updating your eBook, responding to reader feedback, and adapting your marketing strategy.

Writing and publishing an eBook can be a fulfilling and profitable endeavor for authors. By choosing a topic, outlining your eBook, writing and editing your work, designing and converting your eBook, publishing it on a relevant platform, marketing it effectively, and monitoring and adjusting as necessary, you can share your knowledge and creativity with readers around the world.

# Self-Publishing:

The process of publishing and disseminating a book, e-book, or other written work without the help of a formal publishing business is known as self-publishing. Because of technological advancements and the advent of internet markets, it has gained popularity recently.

**These are some important actions to think about while self-publishing:**
Writing your book is the first stage in the self-publishing process. This entails doing your homework, putting your thoughts into order, and writing in an interesting, clear, and succinct manner. To make sure your work is flawless and error-free, editing, and proofreading are also crucial.

Design Your Book: Your book's attractiveness and readability may be affected by its design. This involves selecting fonts, layouts, cover designs, and drawings that complement your brand and appeal to your target market.

Your book has to be converted into a digital format like PDF or EPUB that can be read on electronic devices after it has been written and prepared. Choose a Self-Publication Platform There are several self-publishing options, including Apple iBooks, Barnes & Noble Press, and Amazon Kindle Direct Publishing. It's crucial to do your homework and choose a platform that fits your objectives and target market.

Setting your book's price might be difficult, but it's necessary to take into account the book's length, genre, and market demand. You may get a better notion of the market worth by looking up the costs of comparable books.

After your book has been formatted and priced, it's time to publish it on the self-publishing website of your choice. This involves submitting your book for review, establishing your pricing, and providing your digital materials.

Promote Your Book: In order to reach prospective readers, your book has to be promoted. Social media, email marketing, advertising, and networking with other writers and book lovers are all effective ways to do this.

The sales and reviews of your book should be closely monitored, and any required revisions should be made. This entails modifying your book, reacting to reader comments, and altering your promotional approach.

It is now simpler than ever for writers to share their work with audiences all across the globe thanks to self-publishing. You may take charge of your publishing journey and reach your audience by writing and editing your book, designing and converting it, selecting a self-publishing platform, determining your pricing, releasing your book, promoting it successfully, and monitoring and modifying as required.

# CHAPTER 5 :

## Optimizing Passive Income with Side Jobs,

Today's world offers a wide range of side business alternatives, which are methods to generate additional income outside of your primary work or company. You may be able to reach financial independence and freedom with the aid of these side jobs, which may provide an extra source of money.

**Here are some pointers to help you make the most of your side businesses' passive income:**

The first step in increasing your passive income from side businesses is to choose one that fits your hobbies, abilities, and financial objectives. This might include working as a freelance writer, instructing online, selling digital goods, renting out a home or a room, or making stock or real estate investments.

When deciding on a side business, it's critical to develop a strategy including your objectives, tactics, and timetables. Setting a budget, finding possible clients or consumers, and investigating the market need for your goods or services are all part of this process.

Automate Your Earnings: One advantage of passive income is that it may be generated automatically with little to no work on your side. This may be achieved via a variety of strategies and techniques, including affiliate marketing, advertising, and stock or mutual fund investment, among others.

Use Internet Platforms: With the growth of the gig economy, a variety of online platforms are available that let you generate passive income. These include websites that allow freelancers to find employment, like Upwork or Fiverr, or that let people sell digital goods, like Etsy or Amazon.

Invest in Yourself: It's critical to invest in your abilities and expertise if you want to enhance your side hustle passive revenue. This might be reading books and articles on your side business, participating in seminars or conferences, or taking online courses.

Network and Collaborate: Collaborating and networking with other side hustlers may increase your revenue from passive sources and help you reach a wider audience. This may be done via online forums, social media groups, or live events.

Monitor and Modify: It's critical to keep an eye on your profits and modify your tactics as required. This entails keeping track of your earnings and outlays, evaluating your statistics, and revising your strategy.

Planning carefully, being committed, and persevering are essential to maximizing your passive income from side businesses. You may develop a reliable and lucrative passive income stream that will enable you to meet your financial objectives by picking the correct side hustle, making a strategy, automating your profits, using internet platforms, investing in yourself, networking, and collaborating.

# Renting Your Vehicle :

Your vehicle may be rented out to generate passive income. Why not put your vehicle to work and earn some additional money? Many individuals possess automobiles that they only use sometimes or on the weekends. **Here are some pointers for renting out your automobile and making the most money:**

Choose the correct platform: You may hire out your vehicle on a number of platforms, including Zipcar, Getaround, and Turo. Be sure to conduct your homework and choose the platform that works best for you since each one has different regulations and costs.

Establish the Appropriate Price: It's critical to select the right rental rate by taking into account the brand and model of your vehicle, its age and condition, and local demand. To assist you determine a reasonable price, you may utilize the platform's pricing tool or look for nearby vehicles that are comparable to yours.

Maintain Your Car in Excellent Condition: It's crucial to keep your automobile in good shape if you want to draw in renters and keep up positive evaluations. This covers routine upkeep, cleaning, and required repairs.

Tenants should be rigorously screened before being given a vehicle to rent. Most platforms ask for a driver's license and proof of insurance, but you may also request further details or references if you think it's essential.

Safeguard Yourself And Your Car: When renting out your automobile, be sure you have sufficient insurance coverage. While most platforms include renters insurance, you should additionally check with your own insurance provider to be sure you are protected in the event of an accident or property damage.

Good Communication With Tenants: It's critical to have clear communication with tenants both before and throughout the rental time. This includes giving them directions on how to drive the automobile, outlining the rules for using it, and answering any questions or worries they may have.

Watch Your Income And Make Adjustments As Necessary: To optimize your revenue, keep track of your earnings and alter your rental price as necessary. To promote additional rentals, you may also provide clients who return or rent for extended periods of time incentives.

It may be a terrific way to generate passive money to rent out your automobile, but you need to do your homework and take the essential safety measures to safeguard both your car and yourself. You may establish an effective and lucrative passive income stream by picking the best platform, pricing your vehicle fairly, maintaining it in excellent condition, screening renters, safeguarding yourself and your car, being open and transparent with renters, and keeping track of your revenues...

## Renting Your Residence:

Another excellent strategy to generate passive money is to rent out your house. It's now simpler than ever to rent out your house to visitors and earn money while you're away thanks to the growth of holiday rental sites like Airbnb and Vrbo.

Here are some pointers on how to rent out your house and make as much money as possible:

Choose the best rental strategy: You may utilize a variety of rental tactics when renting out your home, including renting out the full property, a spare room, or a separate unit like a basement apartment or guest house. Every tactic has advantages and disadvantages, so think about which one would work best for your house and way of life.

The location and size of your property, the facilities you provide, and the demand in your region should all be taken into account when determining the appropriate rental price. To assist you to determine a reasonable price, you might look at comparable properties in your neighborhood using rental networks.

Make any required repairs and improvements: Before renting out your house, check to see that it is in excellent shape and that any improvements or repairs have been completed. Making your property more appealing to tenants involves things like repairing leaks, swapping out outdated equipment, and changing the décor.

When renting out your property, make sure that it is clean and clutter-free. All of the rooms will be thoroughly cleaned, all personal stuff will be taken out, and new bedding and towels will be offered to visitors.

Renters should be properly screened before moving into a new rental. Asking for references, confirming their identification and rental history, and outlining your expectations for their stay are all part of this.

Make rules and instructions clear: Provide tenants detailed directions on how to enter your house, utilize any appliances or amenities, and adhere to any laws or regulations throughout their stay.

Employ a property manager: If you lack the time or resources to maintain your rental property on your own, think about hiring a property manager to take care of the regular duties like cleaning, maintenance, and guest relations.

Track your income and make any adjustments: To optimize your revenue, keep track of your earnings and tweak your rental pricing or method as necessary.

To promote additional reservations, you may also provide customers who stay longer or are repeat customers discounts.

In order to protect yourself and your property, it's crucial to conduct your homework and take the required safeguards before renting out your house. You can establish a successful and lucrative passive income source by selecting the best rental strategy, pricing your property correctly, making necessary repairs and improvements, cleaning and decluttering, screening potential tenants, outlining clear instructions and rules, employing a property manager, and keeping track of your earnings.

# Pet-Sitting :

Another fantastic passive income opportunity is pet sitting, particularly if you like taking care of animals. Whether they are going away for a few hours or many weeks, many pet owners require someone to look after their animal pals.

**The following advice will help you launch a pet-sitting company and increase your profits:**

Choose your Services: Determine what kinds of pet-sitting services, such as dog walking, pet feeding, or overnight pet care, you wish to provide. Decide what kinds of pets you feel comfortable taking care of after taking into account your abilities and expertise with various animal species.

Establish your Rates: Do some research on local pet-sitting market pricing and adjust your fees appropriately. Think about things like the service's nature, how long you'll be providing it, and how many animals you'll be looking for.

Promote Your Services: To promote your pet-sitting services, use social media, online ads, and neighborhood bulletin boards. If you want to make it simpler for prospective customers to discover you, think about designing a website or business cards.

Create Strong Connections With Customers: Create strong ties with your customers by being communicative, dependable, and trustworthy. Provide updates and pictures of their dogs while they're gone, and swiftly respond to their comments and questions.

Establish a Network of Referrals: Encourage your customers to recommend your pet-sitting services to their friends and family. You could also want to provide discounts or other rewards for referrals.

Get the Required Certificates And Licenses: To run a pet-sitting company, you may need to receive the necessary certifications or licenses depending on where you reside. To find out what's needed in your region, contact your local government or animal welfare groups.

Defend both you and your clients: For the sake of your customers' safety as well as your own, think about getting liability insurance. Have a strategy in place in case of crises and be sure to have customers sign a contract outlining the terms and conditions of your services.

Pet sitting has the potential to be a satisfying and lucrative passive income stream, but it's crucial to do your homework and take the essential safety measures to safeguard both you and your customers.

You can establish a successful and lucrative passive income source while assisting pet owners in caring for their cherished furry friends by deciding on your services, setting your rates, advertising your services, developing relationships with clients, constructing a network of referrals, getting the required certifications and licenses, and protecting both yourself and your clients.

# House-Sitting :

The luxuries of a home away from home may be enjoyed while house-sitting, which is a terrific way to generate passive income. For a few days or many months, many homeowners require someone to take care of their houses while they are away.

**The following advice will help you launch a house-sitting company and increase your profits:**

Choose your Services: Choose the home-sitting services you wish to provide, such as house inspections, plant watering, or pet care. Choose the sorts of jobs you feel comfortable doing after taking into account your abilities and expertise with various home-related duties.

Establish your Rates: Do some research on the going prices in your neighborhood for house-sitting services, and then adjust your charges. Think about things like the kind of service, how long you'll be house-sitting, and the size of the home.

Promote Your Services: To promote your house-sitting services, utilize social media, online ads, and neighborhood bulletin boards. If you want to make it simpler for prospective customers to discover you, think about designing a website or business cards.

Create Strong Connections With Customers: Create strong ties with your customers by being communicative, dependable, and trustworthy. Provide updates and pictures of their houses and dogs while they are away, as well as immediately respond to their messages and concerns.

Establish a Network of Referrals: Encourage your customers to recommend your house-sitting services to their friends and family. You could also want to provide discounts or other rewards for referrals.

Get the Required Certificates and Licenses: In order to run a house-sitting company, you may need to receive the necessary certifications or licenses depending on where you reside. To learn what is necessary for your region, check with your local government or homeowner organizations.

Consider acquiring liability insurance to safeguard both you and your consumers in case of mishaps or property damage. Have a strategy in place in case of crises and be sure to have customers sign a contract outlining the terms and conditions of your services.

Although house sitting may be a fun and lucrative side hustle, it's crucial to conduct your homework and take the essential safety measures to safeguard both you and your customers. You can build a successful and lucrative source of passive income while taking pleasure in the comforts of a home away from home by deciding on your services, establishing your rates, advertising your services, developing relationships with clients, creating a network of referrals, obtaining necessary certifications and licenses, and protecting yourself and your clients.

# Freelancing :

By providing your talents and services to customers on a project-by-project basis, freelancing is a well-liked method of generating passive money. Freelancers often operate on their own and provide customers that want services like writing, design, programming, and consulting but don't want to recruit a full-time employee.

**The following advice can help you start freelancing and increase your earnings:**

Choose Your Niche: Consider the services you want to provide and the people you want to deal with. Choose a specialty that you are enthusiastic about and that has a market need, taking into account your talents and expertise.

Study the going fees for freelancing services in your expertise and vicinity before establishing your pricing. Take into account elements like your background, area of specialization, and the difficulty of the tasks you'll be working on.

Make a portfolio of your work to demonstrate your abilities and knowledge. Add examples of your greatest work and customer endorsements in your cover letter.

Promote Your Services: To promote your services, use online classifieds, social media, and other marketing platforms. If you want to make it simpler for prospective customers to discover you, think about designing a website or business cards.

Establish Positive Connections With Your Clients: To build positive relationships with your customers, you must be dependable, communicative, and provide high-quality work. Provide fast responses to their messages and questions as well as frequent updates on the status of their projects.

Organize Your Time And Money: To increase your income, organize your time and money well. Keeping track of your income and spending can help you budget for taxes and other costs. To remain on top of deadlines and deliverables, use time management software.

Upsell Your Services: Look for chances to provide more services or broaden the scope of your customers' projects in order to upsell your services to current clients.

In order to safeguard both you and your customers, it's crucial to complete your homework and take the essential steps before beginning a freelance project.

You may develop a successful and lucrative passive income source while working on enjoyable projects by choosing your expertise, establishing your pricing, putting up a portfolio, promoting your services, forming connections with customers, managing your time and money, and upselling your services.

# CHAPTER 6 :

# Money Management Planning :

The art and science of managing your money allow you to reach your financial objectives, accumulate wealth, and lead the life of your dreams. Making wise decisions about how to spend, save, invest, and protect your money is part of this process, as is developing a healthy attitude about money and realizing its importance in your life. Simply defined, effective money management is the key to maximizing your earning potential and securing the future you want.

## Developing A Money Mindset:

To master your money attitude, you must have an empowered and positive connection with money. It necessitates that you recognize, get rid of, and then replace any limiting attitudes or ideas you may have about money with positive and constructive ones. You may change your connection with money and become financially successful by developing a growth mentality and accepting abundance. A critical first step to efficient money management and building the life you want is mastering your money attitude.

## Understanding Your Financial Relationship

Effective money management is built on an understanding of your connection with money. Your upbringing, experiences in life, and cultural beliefs all have an impact on how you see money and how you think, feel, and act toward it. You may spot any unfavorable tendencies or limiting ideas that could be preventing you from reaching financial success by being more aware of how you relate to money. After that, you may try to create a healthy and happier relationship with money, one that supports your objectives and beliefs and gives you the ability to attain financial independence.

# How to Recognize Limiting Beliefs and Get Rid of Them:

The first step to managing your money attitude and being financially successful is recognizing limiting beliefs. Limiting beliefs, such as "I'm not good with money" or "Money is the source of all evil," prevent you from attaining your maximum potential.

These ideas may be engrained deeply and be hard to overcome, but they may be questioned and changed for more powerful, constructive ones. You may alter your connection with money and attain financial prosperity by being aware of your limiting ideas and striving to replace them with empowering affirmations and a growth mentality.

## Developing A Wealthy Mindset:

To handle money effectively and succeed financially, one must have a good money attitude. A growth mentality toward money, where you see money as a tool for abundant creation and goal achievement, is a necessary component of a positive money mindset.

In order to adopt this attitude, you must learn to be grateful for what you already have, refrain from comparing yourself to others, and concentrate on your own development.

You may overcome limiting attitudes, establish sound financial practices, and cultivate a feeling of plenty and satisfaction in your life by developing a positive money mentality.

**Putting Together A Financial Plan**

Effective money management and attaining financial success depend on having a financial plan in place. A financial plan includes setting up a budget, coming up with a strategy for reaching those objectives, and establishing clear, precise, and quantifiable financial targets.

This strategy could include methods for boosting income, controlling debt, and saving and investing. You may get insight into your financial condition, pinpoint areas for improvement, and take concrete efforts toward attaining your financial objectives by developing a financial plan. You may develop money, achieve financial stability, and lead the life you want if you have a sound financial strategy in place.

An effective financial plan must include the establishment of SMART financial objectives. Specific, Measurable, Achievable, Relevant, and Time-bound are all acronyms for SMART goals. There is no space for ambiguity and unambiguous definitions of specific aims. Goals that are quantifiable and measurable allow you to measure your progress and identify whether you've succeeded in achieving them. Based on your present financial status and available resources, achievable objectives are ones that are reasonable and feasible. In line with your beliefs, objectives, and overall financial strategy are relevant goals. Time-bound objectives have a set completion date or schedule, which aids in holding you responsible and concentrating. You can remain motivated, monitor your progress, and succeed financially by creating SMART financial objectives.

## Monitoring Your Spending and Budgeting:

Effective money management includes monitoring your spending and creating a budget. Making a budget entails planning how you will divide your money among different costs and savings targets. You may use this strategy to prioritize your spending, stop overspending, and set aside money for future objectives.
Monitoring your spending patterns can help you spot areas where you could be overspending or where you can make cuts.
You may better understand your financial condition, control your spending, and modify your budget as necessary to reach your financial objectives by keeping track of your costs.
You may live within your means, accumulate money, and attain financial stability by using the budget and cost-monitoring software together.

# How to Create an Emergency Fund:

Effective money management includes having an emergency reserve built up. A reserve of funds placed aside for unforeseen costs like medical bills, auto repairs, or lost income is known as an emergency fund. If you don't have an emergency fund, you could have to use credit cards or loans to pay for these costs, which can result in debt and financial strain. Setting away a percentage of your salary each month in order to accumulate 3-6 months' worth of living costs is the process of creating an emergency fund. You may rest easy knowing that you are ready for unforeseen circumstances and can retain your financial security in the face of difficulty by creating an emergency fund.

# CHAPTER 7 :

# Saving and Investing for Your Future :

Effective money management requires you to save and invest for the future. Saving is putting some of your money away for immediate objectives, such as accumulating an emergency fund or saving for a down payment on a home. Contrarily, investing entails putting your money to work in order to produce wealth and long-term growth.
Depending on your objectives and level of risk tolerance, this may include investing in stocks, bonds, real estate, or other assets.
You may develop wealth, gain financial independence, and create a stable financial future for yourself and your loved ones by setting money aside and investing for the future. Even if you can only invest a modest amount initially, it's crucial to start early and continue investing regularly in order to take advantage of compound interest and optimize your profits over time.

## Understanding Compound Interest's Power:

Effective money management and investment need an understanding of the potential of compound interest. The interest that is accrued on both the principal and any interest that has accumulated over time is known as compound interest. As a result, since interest is generated by interest, your money will rise exponentially over time. The power of compound interest can increase the longer you leave your money invested. For instance, if you purchased $10,000 in a stock that increases on average by 8% annually, after 20 years, even if you didn't contribute any more money, your investment would be worth almost $46,000. By comprehending the power of compound interest, you may use this effective instrument to generate wealth and succeed financially by making wise investment selections.

Making the appropriate investment choices is essential to successful money management and attaining your financial objectives.

Stocks, bonds, mutual funds, exchange-traded funds (ETFs), real estate, and other investment options are only a few of the many accessible kinds. Your financial objectives, level of risk tolerance, and time horizon will determine the best investment alternatives for you.

For instance, you can decide to invest in stocks or real estate for the prospect of larger returns over time if you have a longer time horizon and are okay with more risk.

For greater stability and predictable returns, if you have a shorter time horizon or are more risk-averse, you can decide to invest in bonds or mutual funds.

To reduce risk and increase returns, it's crucial to conduct your homework, get advice from a financial adviser if required, and diversify your portfolio across several asset classes.

You may accomplish your financial objectives and accumulate money over time by selecting the best investment solutions for your particular scenario.

# Your Investing Portfolio Should Be Diversified:

A key tactic for minimizing risk and boosting returns over time is portfolio diversification.

To spread out risk and reduce the effect of any one investment on your whole portfolio, diversification entails investing in a range of various asset types, such as stocks, bonds, real estate, and commodities. You may lower your risk of losing money as a result of circumstances that solely influence one asset class or investment by diversifying your portfolio.

For instance, if all of your investments are in equities and the stock market declines, your portfolio is likely to suffer. The effects of a stock market slump will be less severe if you also have assets in bonds, real estate, and other asset types, however.

To keep your portfolio diversified and in line with your objectives and risk tolerance, it's crucial to examine and rebalance it on a regular basis.

You may minimize risk, and increase rewards, and long-term financial success by diversifying your investment portfolio.

Effective money management requires careful debt and credit management.

Debt may help you reach financial objectives like purchasing a home or establishing a company, but if it's not handled well, it can also become a burden.

Understanding the many forms of debt, such as credit card debt, student loans, and mortgages, is crucial. You should also create a strategy for paying off your obligations on schedule.

Among other things, this may include prioritizing loans with higher interest rates, negotiating lower interest rates or more flexible payment options with lenders, and avoiding taking on additional debt wherever feasible.

In order to obtain loans, credit cards, and other financial goods in the future, it's critical to comprehend how credit works and to have a high credit score.

This might include keeping credit card balances low, paying payments on time, and routinely checking your credit report. You may lessen financial stress, raise your credit score, and eventually reach your financial objectives by managing your debt and credit well.

**Knowledge About Your Credit Score**

**Using Effective Debt Management and Repayment Methods:**

The key to managing your debt and accomplishing your financial objectives is to understand your credit score. A credit score is a three-digit figure that tells lenders and other financial organizations how creditworthy you are.

If you have a good credit score, you are considered a low-risk borrower and are thus more likely to be given credit cards and loans with favorable conditions and reduced interest rates.

On the other side, a poor credit score may make it more challenging to get credit and may lead to increased interest rates and costs.

Keep your credit card balances low, pay your payments on time, and don't apply for too much credit if you want to keep your credit score high.

Moreover, you should routinely check your credit report to make sure it is correct and current.

It's critical to create a debt payback plan that fits your financial circumstances if you have debt.

This can include putting high-interest debt, like credit card debt, first and making additional payments when you can.

You can also think about debt consolidation or negotiating lower interest rates or more flexible payment terms with your creditors.

You may accomplish your financial objectives and create a secure financial future by managing your debt well and keeping a high credit score.

## Prudent Credit Use:

Prudent credit use is a crucial component of good money management. Credit may be a helpful tool for accomplishing financial objectives, like purchasing a home or establishing a company, but if it is not used wisely, it can also result in financial issues.

**Here are some pointers for responsible credit use:**

Be sure you can afford the payments before taking out a loan or applying for a credit card. Just borrow what you can afford to return. Don't borrow more money than you need to, and steer clear of debt with exorbitant interest or fees.

Pay your invoices on time since missed payments may hurt your credit score and cost you money. Ensure that you pay your payments on time every month and if you find yourself unable to do so, speak with your lender to go through your choices.

Have a low credit usage ratio. This refers to how little credit you are really utilizing relative to your credit limit. Maintaining a low credit usage rate may boost your credit score and demonstrate to lenders that you're a trustworthy borrower.

Regularly check your credit report: Make sure your credit report is accurate and current by checking it often. Report any mistakes you see right away to the credit bureau.

Avoid asking for too much credit at once. This might hurt your credit score and make lenders hesitant to provide you with a loan. Don't open too many accounts at once, and only seek credit when you really need it.

You may attain your financial objectives and create a solid financial future by utilizing credit responsibly.

# CHAPTER 8 :

## Making Wise Purchase Choices :

Making wise purchases is a crucial component of efficient money management. Here are some pointers for wise purchase choices:
Create a budget: Determine how much you can spend before making any purchases. You may prevent overspending and avoidable debt by doing this.
Do your homework: To uncover the finest offers and possibilities, do your homework before making a major purchase, such as a vehicle or appliance. Check out reviews and evaluate pricing at other stores.
Avoid making impulsive purchases: Although they might be alluring, they can also result in overspending and regret. Take a step back before making a purchase to determine if you really need the thing or whether it's merely a wish.
Before buying a significant purchase, take into account the long-term expenditures, such as maintenance and repairs. Before making the purchase, be sure you can afford the continuing expenses.
Use coupons and discounts: Before making a purchase, look for coupons and discounts. By utilizing coupons and benefiting from deals and promotions, you may save money.
You may save money, stay out of debt, and reach your financial objectives by making wise purchase selections.
Keeping away from impulsive purchases and regret:
Effective money management includes avoiding impulsive purchases and buyer's regret. These are some suggestions for preventing impulsive purchases and buyer's remorse:
Create a list of the things you need before you go shopping. Keep to the list and refrain from purchasing anything that isn't on it.
If you find something you want to buy, give yourself 24 hours to think about it. You will have more time to consider if you really need the item and whether it is in your price range.
Establish a spending cap: Decide how much you can afford to spend on each shopping trip and adhere to it. You can prevent overpaying and impulsive purchases by doing this.

Avoid shopping when anxious or emotional: Steer clear of shopping when you're stressed or emotional. Emotional purchasing may result in impulsive purchases and regretful purchases.

Analyze your purchases to see if they were wise decisions. Consider if the item fits within your budget and whether you really required it. If you can, return the item if you regret the purchase.

You may save money, stay out of debt, and reach your financial objectives by avoiding impulsive purchases and buyer's remorse.

## Finding the Best Deals and Negotiating Prices:

Finding discounts and negotiating rates are crucial components of sound money management.

**Here are some pointers for finding deals and haggling over prices:**

Do your homework: To get the greatest offers and rates, do your homework before making a buy. Search for discounts, bargains, and special offers. The best price may be found by comparing prices from several merchants.

Don't be hesitant to ask for discounts, particularly when purchasing expensive products. Find out whether the store has any special deals or discounts available for seniors, students, or active military.

Think about purchasing used: Purchasing used goods might be an excellent method to save money. Search for used things at secondhand shops or online.

Price haggling is acceptable when purchasing from an individual vendor, such as one found on Craigslist. Ask the vendor whether they will accept your fair offer.

If you can't obtain the price you want, don't be scared to leave if you can't. There could be alternative chances to purchase the item for a lower cost.

You may save money and reach your financial objectives by looking for deals and haggling over costs.

# Knowing Your Real Ownership Costs:

A crucial component of efficient money management is having a clear understanding of the real cost of ownership. The following advice will help you comprehend the real cost of ownership:

Take into account all costs: When purchasing an item, take into account all the expenses related to owning it. This covers the cost of the original purchase as well as recurring expenses like upkeep, repairs, and insurance.

Take a broad view: When contrasting the costs of various things, take a broad view. If an inexpensive item requires more frequent maintenance or repairs, it can wind up costing you more in the long term.

Think about the resale value before making a large-ticket purchase. In the long term, a higher-quality item could be a better investment because of its potential for a greater resale value.

While purchasing an object, take longevity into account. A product of superior quality could last longer, with fewer replacements and repairs.

Making more informed purchase selections can help you save money over time by helping you to grasp the real cost of ownership.

## Defending Your Money:

Safeguarding your finances involves taking the necessary procedures and precautions to keep your money, property, and personal information secure against theft, fraud, and unauthorized access.

In order to avoid financial losses and safeguard your financial security, entails being aware of possible dangers and taking preventative action.

Here are some pointers for safeguarding your money:

Employ secure passwords: For your online accounts, use secure passwords and update them often. Employ a mix of symbols, numerals, and capital and lowercase characters.

Check your accounts often for any strange activity.

This includes your bank and credit card accounts. All unlawful transactions must be reported right away.

Use two-factor authentication: Whenever feasible, use two-factor authentication for your online accounts. This adds an additional level of security.

Your social security number, birth date, and bank information are all examples of personal information that should be handled with caution. Share this information only with people you can trust and only when necessary.

Safeguard your gadgets: Install antivirus software on your computer, phone, and other devices, and keep it updated with the most recent security updates.

Before discarding any important papers, including credit card statements, bank statements, and other financial records, shred them.

You can prevent fraud and identity theft and reach your financial objectives by safeguarding your money.

# Keeping Your Personal Information and Identity Safe:

Protecting your money and safeguarding your financial security need you to take steps to secure your identity and personal information.

**Here are some pointers for protecting your identity and private data:**
Your social security number, birth date, and bank information are all examples of personal information that should be handled with caution. Share this information only with people you can trust and only when necessary.

Employ secure passwords: For your online accounts, use secure passwords and update them often. Employ a mix of symbols, numerals, and capital and lowercase characters.

Safeguard your gadgets: Install antivirus software on your computer, phone, and other devices, and keep it updated with the most recent security updates.

Phishing schemes should be avoided: Be suspicious of emails or texts that want personal information or money. These might be phishing schemes intended to steal your personal information.

Do a credit report check: Check your credit report often for any unusual activities. All unlawful transactions must be reported right away.

Use two-factor authentication: Whenever feasible, use two-factor authentication for your online accounts. This adds an additional level of security.

You may defend against identity theft, fraud, and other financial losses by protecting your identity and personal information. This may assist you in maintaining and achieving your long-term financial objectives.

Selecting the Best Insurance Plans Preparing an Estate and Leaving a Legacy:

The correct insurance policy selection, estate planning, and legacy creation are all crucial elements of successful financial planning.

**Here is a quick synopsis of each:**
The correct insurance plans may provide financial security in the case of unforeseen circumstances like sickness, incapacity, or death. It's critical to choose the appropriate insurance plans for your requirements, including those for life, health, disability, and other types of insurance.

Planning your estate entails making arrangements for the disposition of your assets after your passing. Making a will, establishing trusts, and naming beneficiaries for your retirement accounts and other assets are some examples of how to do this.

Building a legacy is creating a strategy for transferring your ideals, convictions, and financial assets to future generations. This might include making donations to charities, establishing a family foundation, and other tactics.

You may make sure that your financial resources are utilized in accordance with your preferences and care for your loved ones and future generations by picking the appropriate insurance products, drafting an estate plan, and leaving a legacy. It's crucial to collaborate with a financial planner or attorney to create a thorough strategy that addresses your unique requirements and aspirations.

## Increasing Wealth and Volunteering:

Financial planning includes two crucial elements that may help you attain both financial success and personal fulfillment: building wealth and giving back. Here is a quick synopsis of each:

Making a long-term financial strategy in order to expand your assets and raise your net worth over time is the first step in building wealth. This might include tactics like putting money aside for retirement and managing debt wisely, as well as investing in stocks, bonds, and other assets.

Giving back entails using your financial resources to aid issues and organizations you value. Giving to charities, offering your time and talents, and assisting small companies and community groups are some examples of this.

You may have a beneficial effect on both your financial future and the world around you by accumulating money and giving back. Finding strategies to include both of these objectives in your financial strategy and striking a balance between them is crucial. You may create an all-encompassing strategy that supports your principles and objectives by consulting with a financial planner or adviser.

## Providing for Your Neighborhood and Others:

Giving back to your community and the world at large is a crucial component of financial planning that may bring both personal satisfaction and have a good effect on the environment. Here are some ideas for charitable giving:

Giving to charity: Giving to charity is contributing money or other resources to organizations and causes you support. This might include giving to regional charities, assisting foreign groups, and contributing to relief efforts for natural disasters.

Volunteering: Volunteering is lending your time and talents to organizations and causes you support. This might include giving your time to a nearby charity, joining a nonprofit board, or offering your talents for free to help neighborhood projects.

Investing in firms and funds that promote good social and environmental results and connect with your beliefs is known as socially responsible investment.

Philanthropic endeavors: To assist the issues and organizations you are passionate about, you might start your own charity organization or foundation.

You may have a positive influence on the world around you and contribute to the greater good by giving back to your town and beyond. Finding charitable endeavors that support your beliefs and objectives is crucial. You should also work with a financial planner or adviser to include charitable giving in your financial strategy.

## Developing Family Wealth:

Developing assets and money that can be handed down from one generation to the next is referred to as building generational wealth. It entails putting in place financial habits and tactics that support leaving a legacy of stability and security for a family's future generations.

**The following are some methods for creating generational wealth:**
Investing in assets that increase in value over time may serve as a solid basis for creating generational wealth. Examples of such assets include real estate, stocks, and companies.

The process of setting up a family trust: A family trust is a legal body that may keep and manage assets for the benefit of your family members. You may make sure that your money is tax-efficiently handed down to subsequent generations by setting up a family trust.

Creating a family office: A family office is a group of experts who can handle the financial assets of your family, including investments, taxes, and estate planning. Your money may be properly and efficiently handled if a family office is established.

Teaching the next generation about money may help them get the information and abilities they need to handle their own finances and carry on the family's tradition of accumulating wealth.

Building generational wealth may help you leave your family with a secure financial future for many generations to come. It's crucial to collaborate with a financial planner or adviser to create a thorough strategy that is in line with your objectives and principles.

# Conclusion

In conclusion, there are several methods to generate passive income from side businesses, whether you want to rent out your vehicle or residence, provide pet or house-sitting services, market your creative works, or freelance. Finding a side company that fits your interests and abilities and approaching it with a business attitude are the keys to success.

You may establish a lucrative and long-lasting passive income stream that supports your full-time work or offers financial security on its own by adopting a sound plan, selling your services successfully, cultivating relationships with customers, and managing your time and money sensibly. To optimize your profits and accomplish your objectives, keep in mind to complete your study, maintain organization, and be persistent in your efforts.

**Steps for Selecting the Best Passive Income Idea for You**

It's crucial to choose the best passive income strategy for you after researching several options. The following actions will assist you in making that choice:

Think about your hobbies and skills: Choose a passive income concept that fits with your hobbies and talents. This will make it simpler for you to maintain motivation and succeed in your chosen endeavor.

Establish your financial objectives: Define your desired level of passive income and establish attainable financial objectives. When you strive to reach your target income level, this will support your ability to remain motivated and focused.

Analyze the market and do market research to see if there is a market for the notion of passive income you have selected. Determine chances for differentiation and innovation by analyzing the competition.

Assess the possible risks and advantages of your selected passive income plan, taking into account the initial investment, recurring expenses, and prospective returns. To make an educated choice, thoroughly weigh the advantages and dangers.

Start small and expand: As you acquire expertise and success, start with a modest idea or investment and progressively expand. You can reduce risk and increase profits over time by doing this.

Be persistent and patient since creating an effective passive income stream takes time. In your efforts, be patient and tenacious, and don't give up if you don't get results right away.

You can pick the best passive income idea for you and create a successful and enduring passive income source by taking into account your skills and interests, setting realistic financial goals, researching the market, assessing the potential risks and rewards, starting small, and scaling up, and being patient and persistent. Keep in mind that there is no one solution that suits all situations and that what works for one person may not work for you. Hence, take your time, do your research, and choose the passive income opportunity that best suits your objectives and dreams.

## Glossary of Terms for Passive Income

A dictionary of terminology pertaining to passive income is provided below:
Income obtained without actively participating in a company or trade.
A second job or additional source of income in addition to one's main work.
Intellectual property that may be leased or sold for passive revenue, such as photographs, music, or artwork.
Royalties: Sums paid to an author or owner of intellectual property in exchange for using their creation.
Affiliate marketing is a kind of marketing where a person promotes another person's product in exchange for a cut of any sales that arise.
Online purchasing and selling of products and services are known as e-commerce.
Online course: A digital course that is available for purchase and enrollment by anyone, anywhere.
Self-publishing is the process of independently releasing a book, e-book, or other written work.
Stock images: Images that have a license for commercial use and may be bought and sold again.
Licensing: A contract in which a creator authorizes the use of their intellectual property by a third party.
Freelancing: Acting as an independent contractor to provide services to customers on a project-by-project basis.
Upselling: Adding more services or broadening the scope of an ongoing project to boost sales.
A synchronization license is a permit that allows the use of a certain song in a film or other kind of media production.
A performance license is needed to play copyrighted music in public settings like concerts and radio broadcasts.

A reliable and ongoing source of passive income is referred to as a passive income stream.

Budget: A plan for how you will spend your money over a specific period of time, usually a month.

Income: Money earned from work or investments.

Expenses: The money spent on goods and services, such as rent, food, utilities, transportation, and entertainment.

Savings: Money set aside for future use, such as an emergency fund or retirement savings.

Debt: Money owed to others, such as credit card debt or a mortgage.

Credit Score: A numerical rating used by lenders to determine your creditworthiness, based on your history of borrowing and repaying money.

Interest: The amount of money charged by lenders for borrowing money.

Investing: The process of putting money into stocks, bonds, or other assets in the hopes of generating a profit.

Retirement Planning: The process of saving and investing money to ensure financial security during retirement.

Financial Goals: Specific objectives for how you want to manage your money, such as saving for a down payment on a house or paying off debt.

www.ingramcontent.com/pod-product-compliance
Lightning Source LLC
Chambersburg PA
CBHW071111220526
45467CB00004B/1800